THE
BUSINESS PLANNING
POCKETBOOK

By Neil Russell-Jones

Drawings by Phil Hailstone

"Excellent - clear, concise and very practical."
Kevin Jones, Group Planning Executive, Norwich

"Excellent introduction to the basics of planning. Se
those who are new to the world of business plannin
Nicholas Beazley, Head of Strategic Planning, BU

Published by:
Management Pocketbooks Ltd
Laurel House, Station Approach, Alresford, Hants SO24 9JH, U.K.
Tel: +44 (0)1962 735573   Fax: +44 (0)1962 733637
E-mail: sales@pocketbook.co.uk
Website: www.pocketbook.co.uk

This edition published 1998.   Reprinted 1999, 2000, 2002, 2004.

© Neil Russell-Jones 1998

ISBN 1 870471 58 X

Coventry University

British Library Cataloguing-in-Publication Data – A catalogue record for this book is available from the British Library.

Design, typesetting and graphics by **efex Ltd.**   Printed in U.K.

CONTENTS

INTRODUCTION

DEFINITION

Planning is a feature of everyday living - whether at home or in business. Without it our lives would be totally chaotic and random.

Plans vary from imprecise vague statements to thick volumes prepared over a long period.

Some are useful; others a waste of time. Very few remain unaltered.

People are frequently asked to prepare a plan with no guidance at all, and the result often falls short of expectations.

DEFINITION

Richard Hannay, the hero of many of John Buchan's books, had a companion who was a South African Boer - Peter Pienaar. Whenever he was faced with a seemingly impossible situation he would say 'Ik shall een plaan mak' - I shall make a plan. He would subsequently carry out the task successfully.

Planning is taking time to:

- Consider the possibilities that might arise as a result of something that you wish to do
- Understand the consequences that arise, and
- Develop actions to counter them or to maximise opportunities

WHO SHOULD USE THIS BOOK?

Planning takes place in all organisations in some form or other, whether it be formal or informal, and at a variety of levels. Most planning is carried out by middle management in larger organisations, and by people who run their own businesses (proprietors, sole traders, partners or directors of small and medium sized organisations).

If you are in a department or business unit and have to prepare a plan, then this book will help you understand the components and do's and don't's of planning. Those engaged in business on their own behalf will also find it useful.

Some parts of the book may be more appropriate to businesses than, for example, to head office departments, but will fill out the wider background for the latter.

WHO SHOULD USE THIS BOOK?

The Business Planning Pocketbook concentrates on what you need to do to produce a plan. It includes both the theory and the practical aspects.

Whatever your situation, the basic planning process itself is fundamentally the same - it is just the format and style of development, and sometimes execution, that differ. There may be different front ends to the process, and different issues to consider, but in essence plans are all the same: **a detailed outline of something that is going to happen.**

There is also a body of people engaged in planning at a corporate level. (This is usually termed corporate or strategic planning.) This book, whilst touching on strategic planning by way of context, is not really for them.

CORPORATE PLANNING

It is important to differentiate between planning that takes place at the highest level and that which takes place within an organisation. The former may be referred to as **'corporate planning'**, and is usually found in large organisations; whilst the latter may be referred to as **'business planning'**.

Corporate planning is concerned with planning for the organisation as a whole - not for the whole organisation; and it is important to understand the difference.

Any organisation trying to plan for the whole will not succeed, due both to the workloads and the immense number of variables for consideration. (A good analogy is with the former Command Economies where they tried to plan entire countries centrally - with all too familiar failures.)

Corporate planning is about deciding corporate goals and then developing corporate strategies to achieve these. This might take several years and, therefore, it is by nature a long-term view.

BUSINESS PLANNING

Business planning is concerned with what is going to be done **now** to achieve targets and goals.

It sits, therefore, at the tactical level rather than the strategic.

It is necessarily short-term in outlook; but can nevertheless span a number of years. For example, building a ship or a petroleum cracking plant might take several years to complete, but this would not be a corporate plan, merely one component of a business plan (although for some firms it might be a very large component).

Generally, business plans take a one year horizon, although they will sit within the long-term framework established at a corporate level.

VISIONS, STRATEGIES & PLANS

It is important to understand the difference between a vision,
a strategy and a plan. People often use the terms interchangeably
which leads to confusion. In a business sense, however:

- A **vision** is the long-term view or ideal that
  drives the organisation

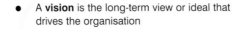

- The **strategy** is the articulation of the vision into
  practical reality, given the actual situation

- The **plan** is the tactical means of achieving the
  strategy - the actions that need to be taken

VISION, STRATEGIES & PLANS
TIMESCALES

VISION	10-20+ years
STRATEGY	3-5 years
PLANS	1 year

- The vision shapes the strategy, which in turn shapes the plans that support it

- The time horizon decreases as you descend, with plans typically looking only one year out

- Certainty generally increases as the time horizon reduces

VISION, STRATEGIES & PLANS

- The vision and strategy are only the pinnacle of the planning process, with most of the work and content below them
- The strategy will probably be supported by several plans within the strategic context; including business unit plans and support unit plans, all of which are linked through the strategy
- Some plans (HR, marketing, IT) will cut across the organisation
- To be of any use, of course, they must lead to definite action

VISIONS

Many of the most successful organisations can trace their success to the fact that they have a clear vision which is understood by all employees, customers and, often, suppliers.

Examples of this include:

John Lewis Partnership
(a UK department store chain) whose motto is 'Never Knowingly Undersold'

Coca-Cola
(a US soft drink manufacturer) whose vision was originally that US GI's should be able to buy a Coke anywhere in the world; currently the most successful brand in the world

Wedgwood
(a UK china manufacturer) whose philanthropic founder Josiah Wedgwood had a vision that ordinary people should be able to buy good crockery at low prices

Microsoft
(a US software company) whose vision is a PC on every desk

STRATEGIES

A strategy is the articulation of the vision in terms that can be easily understood by everyone, although still at a high level.

It takes the vision, which is often on a rather lofty plane, and puts borders around it in terms of what it means for the company.

This is usually expressed through shared goals with customers and 'stakeholders', as well as goals for excellence.

These are the things at which the organisation must excel and, therefore, which will shape the organisation and its internal working and actions.

STRATEGIES

The goals will have a set of measures attached to each to quantify what they mean.

Examples could be:

- Return on assets of 3%
- Cost/income ratios of 45%
- Staff turnover below 5%
- Share price a multiple of 15 times earnings, etc

The goals and measures provide the internal strategic framework within which to plan.

When coupled with the external environment, a series of actions can then be developed to carry out the strategy - **THE PLAN.**

PLANS

Plans are the tactical means of implementing strategy and achieving objectives.

A plan sets out exactly:

- What needs to be done
- By whom, and
- When

It focuses on the **How** rather than the **What**.

The rest of the book will concentrate on this aspect.

PLANNING THEORY

PLANNING THEORY

INTRODUCTION

There is a plethora of writing about planning theory, but there are a few things that all are agreed on:

- Planning is data driven

- You must have enough information to make decisions, but no more than is sufficient (avoid paralysis analysis)

- It is more likely that a plan will work if those who have to carry it out are involved in its conception and development

- It should set out a firm structure but it must not be too rigid and it should have flexibility to adapt to changing circumstances

- Progress must be monitored against the plan

WHAT IS A PLAN?

- A plan can be defined as a set of instructions:
  - to someone
  - to do something
  - in a certain manner
  - within a given timescale, and
  - with a finite set of resources
- It designs and precedes action, but is not action
- It helps you fit a set of (possibly) random events into a framework; this enables you to visualise, and therefore make sense of, something intangible and so cope better with it
- It breaks a large undertaking up into a set of discrete measurable tasks

ORDER FOR
GETTING UP
1. GET OUT OF BED
2. SHOWER
3. CLEAN TEETH
4. SHAVE
5. BREAKFAST
6. GET DRESSED
7. LEAVE FOR WORK

PLANNING THEORY

WHAT IS A PLAN?

A plan:
- Has objectives which can be measured
- Answers questions that stakeholders should be asking
- Builds in options and contingencies
- Identifies and quantifies risks
- Sets out how to minimise those risks or the adverse consequences that might arise from them
- Allows progress to be measured

Planning involves:
- Management and executive time and input
- Commitment
- Cost
- Research
- Assumptions

Therefore, it is important to get it right (or less wrong than the opposition)!

PLANNING THEORY

WHY PLAN?

For some people planning is second nature: for others it is quite the reverse.
The dangers of poor planning will be more obvious in some environments than others.
The greatest military victories were almost always won where they had been planned thoroughly and all eventualities considered.

Planning gives:

- Certainty
- Measures
- Confidence
- A route map
- Evidence to others of forethought

PLANNING THEORY

WHY PLAN?

Planning will help you to:

- Shape your thoughts
- Think through scenarios and implications
- Ensure that points are not missed
- Demonstrate business control
- Identify weaknesses and opportunities
- Examine the risk of an action/set of actions against the return
- Provide a tool to communicate ideas to third parties (superiors, subordinates, lenders, suppliers, owners, etc)

WHY PLAN?

Many people will say that planning is unnecessary and that they get by without it.

This may be fine in some circumstances, but where the environment is complex it will result in failure.

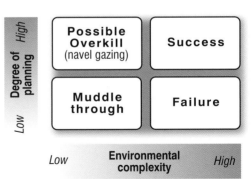

KNOW YOUR AUDIENCE

Plans are produced for several different reasons and for different people. Each organisation has needs that are unique to it, as well as a unique set of stakeholders (those who have an interest in the outcomes of its operations).

The major stakeholders can include some or all of:

- Shareholders
- Lenders
- Creditors
- Potential investors
- Government (tax)
- The Community, in some cases

PLANNING THEORY

KNOW YOUR AUDIENCE

Planner	Audience includes:
● Sole trader	● Bank manager, creditors, taxman, auditors
● Partnership	● Fellow partners, staff, bank managers, creditors, professional body, taxman, auditors
● Small company	● Directors, creditors, staff, bank manager, taxman, auditors
● Department/unit in an organisation	● Head of department/unit, other departments/units, superiors, auditors, group planning, accounts department

PLANNING THEORY

ELEMENTS OF A PLAN

There is no magic formula for the contents of a plan and, whilst there are some key items that must be present, levels of details will differ with organisational needs. Essential elements include:

- Internal situation analysis of your organisation/division/department/unit

- External analysis of your market and competition

- Product and service offerings description

- Targets going forward

- A budget for expenditure and resources

- Economic forecasts

- 'What if?' analysis

These elements demonstrate adequate research, analysis and thought in preparing the plan.

PLANNING STYLES

Planning styles differ from organisation to organisation. Example styles include:

- **Top-down** where the initial plan is set centrally

- **Bottom-up** where contributions are aggregated in stages

- A **blend** of these two where guidelines are set centrally along with macro-economic analysis, and units are allowed to prepare their own plans within this framework

- **Informal planning**

- **Numbers based** (traditional)

- **Scenario based**

- **Economic Value Analysis**

- **Balanced scorecard**

PLANNING STYLES

TOP DOWN

This type was probably the most common in organisations where formal planning processes existed, although now many others are being used.

Plans are set centrally and cascade down the organisation. They are often arrived at without proper consultation and discussion, setting arbitrary targets. Those receiving the plan and its targets are, for the most part, only rarely consulted and end up trying to achieve something that they have neither bought into nor developed.

Not surprisingly, this type of planning is not effective, especially if the planners do not take into account the circumstances of those executing the plans.

A theoretical set of targets might be unachievable in practice, and cause many problems for those at the sharp end.

PLANNING STYLES

BOTTOM UP

This type of planning starts with the lowest unit that plans and then aggregates the plans together to yield, ultimately, the final plan for the whole organisation.

A set of guidelines is usually established (though not always), and units produce their own plans within this framework. An aggregation process will ensure consistency of output, reducing in detail as it flows up the organisation.

This method involves everybody and takes their input, but it can take a long time and be very repetitive.

- Often very numbers based - strong focus on budgets
- Often leads to conflict as the units try to set themselves unduly easy targets that do not equate with what the organisation needs

PLANNING STYLES

BLEND

This is a combination of the two preceding styles. A general plan is constructed at the top level and then merged with the results of a bottom-up exercise.

Usually there is a central co-ordinating body which conducts research, gives macro-economic forecasts and sets general guidelines as well as the framework. It acts as the aggregating and the initial challenging unit.

The results are then reviewed, challenged, altered and consolidated.

Economic capital planning often takes this approach.

PLANNING STYLES

INFORMAL PLANNING

This is usually found in smaller and medium sized organisations where, for example, the directors meet and discuss next year's targets and goals. It is often found in successful entrepreneurial organisations. The key advantage is that it is not a time-consuming exercise, and is very flexible.

Problems arise, however, when the business environment becomes more complex, and this type of planning proves inadequate for control and measurement.

This can often have disastrous consequences for firms unless they move smoothly to other, more disciplined, methods of planning.

PLANNING STYLES

NUMBERS BASED

Probably the most common style of all, and may be used in conjunction with another method. It gives great comfort to people as, by concentrating on the quantitative rather than the qualitative, it appears more certain. It is easier to produce a cashflow than to understand the likelihood of people to prefer your product, but you can lose sight of the bigger picture.

One of the criticisms levelled against GEC in the latter part of Arnold Weinstock's reign was that planning was purely based on cashflow, ignoring other aspects, and that this led to its lack of vision.

All plans, of course, involve an element of numerical analysis, but relying wholly on numbers has largely been discredited now and a broader perspective is more commonly taken.

PLANNING STYLES

SCENARIO BASED

A very advanced type of planning, of which Shell is perhaps one of the leading exponents. It usually takes a very much longer 'time horizon' than other forms of planning and lays great emphasis on 'what ifs'.

It involves agreeing future likely scenarios and then analysing the impact on the business, and the action required to counter adverse consequences. These scenarios can then be weighted by probability. A best-fit path can then be charted between the most likely to occur, with contingency plans for action should one scenario develop strongly.

It is an excellent method of quantifying uncertainty, but often involves the use of very complex models and analysis techniques looking quite far into the future. It is, therefore, inappropriate for most businesses and is more strategic than tactical.

Where large capital investments are planned, however, this method can yield substantial benefits over others.

PLANNING THEORY

PLANNING STYLES
ECONOMIC VALUE ADDED

 This approach is heavily dependent on numbers. It focuses on the return on the capital used by the business, less the cost of that capital. This is usually calculated as a Weighted Average Cost of Capital (equity and debt) [WACC]. It is used by, inter alia, Coca-Cola, Siemens, Procter & Gamble and many others.

The key determinant is whether the activities create value over and above the cost of capital, or consume or destroy value. In other words, do they increase the value of the organisation at the end of the year?

Planning is carried out to ensure that activities beat this measure. Those using it claim heady success in increased business focus. It has shown some surprising results in many organisations; challenging some long-cherished assumptions about where true value is generated.

It started in the USA then spread to the UK. It has latterly found a degree of reluctant acceptance in continental Europe as private shareholders have become more prominent. It is particularly useful in large organisations with many business units.

PLANNING STYLES

BALANCED SCORECARD

This approach is an attempt to blend together quantitative numerical analysis with qualitative analysis of other elements that are important to organisations, such as:

- The customer's perspective - what the customer thinks of us; how to improve loyalty
- The internal perspective - what we must excel at, eg: employee skills
- Finance - what our targets must be, eg; cost/income ratio, return on assets, return on capital, profit
- Long-term survival - looking to the future and innovating to create extra value

It is a measure that will drive the shape of all plans, as each must address all four aspects of the scorecard.

It can be difficult to use in practice, however, and can cause confusion if inadequately explained.

WHICH STYLE?

Which planning
style is suited to
your organisation?

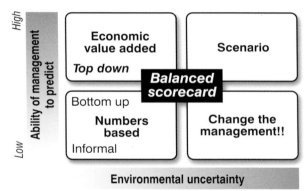

Economic value added *Top down*	**Scenario**	
	Balanced scorecard	
Bottom up **Numbers based** Informal	**Change the management!!**	

Ability of management to predict — High / Low

Environmental uncertainty

Low — High

PLANNING PROCESS

INTRODUCTION

The planning process is a sequence of steps that are followed in order to produce a plan, which is the ultimate output. It involves analysis and development of conclusions, as well as actions.

A typical planning process involves the following steps:

1 Situation analysis
2 External analysis
3 Gap analysis
4 Action development
5 Resource assessment
6 Target setting
7 Financial modelling

PLANNING PROCESS

1: SITUATION ANALYSIS

Internally focused:

Understanding:

- Where you are
- How you got there
- What you have
- What is missing

Strengths
Weaknesses
Historical performance
Trends
Resources

PLANNING PROCESS

1: SITUATION ANALYSIS

This is the analysis of your own particular organisation or unit and would include:

- A historical analysis of your own situation, ie: what you have accomplished to date
- The trends in that accomplishment, highlighting:
  - Areas in which you feel you are relatively strong
  - The degree of that strength
  - Reasons why (key elements of success)
  - Areas where you feel that you are weaker
  - The degree of weakness
  - Reasons why
  - Key resources/requirements

2: EXTERNAL ANALYSIS

Outward looking:

Who is out there?

What are they doing?

What are the trends?

How will it affect you?

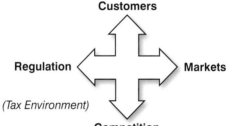

Customers

Regulation — **Markets**

(Tax Environment)

Competition

Even internal
departments (HR, IT)
have customers, although
there may be no direct competition.
Of course, **every** department should
be supporting the organisation's drive to service its customers.

PLANNING PROCESS

2: EXTERNAL ANALYSIS

An analysis of forces outside your organisation which will impact on your plans.
This will include markets, competition, customers, regulation, tax and environment.

Markets

- What is happening in them?
- Where do you fit in?
- What are the trends?
- Are there opportunities there?
- Entry/exit barriers
- How can your unit support the organisation here?

2: EXTERNAL ANALYSIS

Competition

- Who are the current competitors?
- Who might they be in the future?
- What are their products?
- How are they competing (price, service, quality, marketing)?
- How do they distribute?

Tax

- How important is it to you? (clever tax planning can save £ millions for large organisations)
- Are there advantages in bringing some services in-house?

2: EXTERNAL ANALYSIS

Customers

- Who are they?

- Where are they?

- How do you communicate
  to them?

- Which are the key segments
  (Pareto analysis: those that
  deliver the highest proportion
  of value)?

- What are their needs and
  (how) are they changing?

- Who will be the future
  customers?

PLANNING PROCESS

2: EXTERNAL ANALYSIS

Regulation

- What are the current regulations affecting your business (there could be several levels of these, eg: national, federal, global)?
- Are you compliant - if not how/when will you be?
- How might they change?
- What are the implications for you?

Environment

- How important is this consideration to you, your customers, your stakeholders?
- How will it affect you, eg:
  - will it change your costs?
    your suppliers?
  - are there legal implications?

3: GAP ANALYSIS

Now look at the external analysis in conjunction with your internal situation, and highlight areas where you are relatively strong and those which need development/action. Prioritise the points by reference to your competition.

The higher the priority and the greater the gap, the greater the emphasis on the change.

Key points for analysis - difference between where you are and where you want to be indicates development need

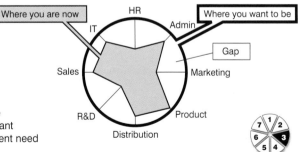

4: ACTION DEVELOPMENT

Having identified the gaps, you need to take action to close them. This involves developing those areas where you are weak, and maintaining and enhancing those where you are strong:

- If you identify that your products are deficient, then you must produce a plan to improve existing ones or to introduce new ones

- Where technology is crucial to success you must develop a plan to bring your organisation up to competitors' levels or, better still, one step ahead

- If your staff have the wrong skills or the wrong training this must be addressed

All in the context of the strategic goals, of course.

PLANNING PROCESS

5: RESOURCE ASSESSMENT

Once you have completed the action development stage, you can examine what resources you will need. The gap analysis will have highlighted some areas, which will have been expanded during the action development. This stage will be specific and will focus on:

- **People** - management, staff, specialists, external resources
- **Fixed assets** - plant, machinery, buildings
- **IT** - hardware, software, linkages
- **Distribution** - what sort, outlets, remote, agents, electronic
- **Finance** - the money needed to achieve the plan, high level budget, possible type of finance

PLANNING PROCESS

5: RESOURCE ASSESSMENT
PEOPLE

The key questions to be answered include:

- How many people do you need?
- What skills do they require?
- What training is required?
- What recruitment is needed, when?
- What career development must be undertaken?
- How will this be managed?

Manpower Planning

5: RESOURCE ASSESSMENT

FIXED ASSETS

Fixed assets are those assets used to produce the outputs: plant, machinery, land and buildings, etc.

- What do we have?

- Are they right?

- What do we need if not?

- Can we dispose of those unwanted?

- Are depreciation levels right?
  (The type of depreciation chosen can affect corporate results)

- Are we receiving the right rate of return on them
  (are we 'sweating' them)?

5: RESOURCE ASSESSMENT

INFORMATION TECHNOLOGY

Nowadays this is critical to almost all businesses. Often in the past IT departments were out of proportion with the organisation, but with increased IT literacy of management this is less so than before.

IT must support the business and not be a means to its own end. It should be controlled rigidly by the business. Key questions for inclusion in the IT strategy part of the plan include:

- What do we have?
- Does it support the business?
- What is its life? (IT projects are often measured in years)
- Is it compliant?
- Is the plan still going to deliver meaningful IT support to the business?
    - legacy systems (ageing systems which need to be replaced)
    - technology obsolescence

5: RESOURCE ASSESSMENT

DISTRIBUTION

How products/services are distributed to customers is a critical part of strategic planning, and the following questions need to be considered fully:

- Which distribution channels should we use to maximise product outreach?
- Which do we use currently?
- What are the relative channel costs against their respective returns?
- How do we control channels, eg: the internet, where purchases tend to be driven by price rather than brand, and the product suppliers are just icons, with no direct contact with the customer.
- Which will be the future channels?
- What impact will this have on head office departments?

5: RESOURCE ASSESSMENT

DISTRIBUTION CHANNELS

Distribution channels are changing fast

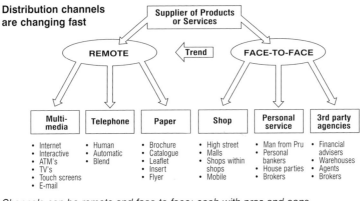

Supplier of Products or Services

REMOTE ← Trend ← FACE-TO-FACE

Multi-media	Telephone	Paper	Shop	Personal service	3rd party agencies
• Internet	• Human	• Brochure	• High street	• Man from Pru	• Financial advisers
• Interactive	• Automatic	• Catalogue	• Malls	• Personal bankers	• Warehouses
• ATM's	• Blend	• Leaflet	• Shops within shops	• House parties	• Agents
• TV's		• Insert	• Mobile	• Brokers	• Brokers
• Touch screens		• Flyer			
• E-mail					

Channels can be remote and face-to-face; each with pros and cons.

5: RESOURCE ASSESSMENT

FINANCE

Finance is the oil of the business engine - without it the firm will grind to a halt.

The key issue is to maximise capital availability against cost and return. Specifically:

- Do we have the right amount of capital for the business plan?
- Is it the right sort - investment v debt; what gearing does it give us?
  - what is the average cost of funds of the business (known as the Weighted Average Cost of Capital or WACC)?
  - what are the implications for payments (dividends v interest)?
- Does the duration of the capital match the expected expenditure and return?

Where capital is allocated to all units these questions are of fundamental importance.

5: RESOURCE ASSESSMENT
FINANCE: GEARING ANALYSIS

debt   **equity**

debt   **equity**

Highly geared company benefits during times of growth as debt is usually cheaper than equity, but suffers in recession as interest payments must always be met.

Company with more balanced debt/equity ratio benefits during recession as dividend payments can be deferred; in times of boom pays out more in dividends, but can attract capital.

5: RESOURCE ASSESSMENT

BUDGETING

Whatever type of planning style is used, it will always be underpinned by a budget.

This is an assessment of likely flows of cash, income and profit for the next year.

If you are in business you will almost certainly have been involved with a budget, whether as someone suffering from its constraints, as a developer of a budget, or even as a management accountant or analyst measuring variances against them.

Despite their bad reputation they are a valuable management tool for controlling business and results.

In poorly managed organisations budgets often take the place of plans, which is very short-term and misleads management into thinking that they are in control.

6: TARGET SETTING

Every plan must contain targets so that you can measure progress and, ultimately, the success of the plan. The targets may be **quantitative** or **qualitative** and typically will include:

- Financial returns
- Costs (absolute or relative)
- Market share
- Manpower
- Sales/volume of business
- Growth
- Customer satisfaction
- Quality of outputs

Where goals have been set, or a balanced scorecard is in use, the targets will be linked back to these.

7: FINANCIAL MODELLING

It is impossible to get away without looking at the financial aspects of a plan. Finance is critical to any business and, in particular, the key is sustainable cashflow.
An organisation, even if unprofitable, can keep going for a long time, provided it can generate sufficient cash to meet its bills as they fall due.
A profitable company that cannot raise cash will go out of business.

You need cash to:

- Pay staff
- Purchase raw materials (settle creditors)
- Pay for consumables
- Invest in assets
- Pay dividends
- Pay tax
- Repay debt

7: FINANCIAL MODELLING

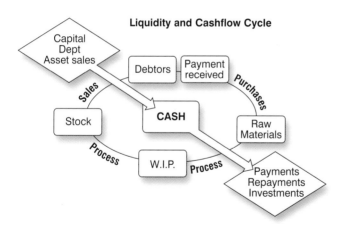

Liquidity and Cashflow Cycle

Capital
Dept
Asset sales

Debtors — Payment received

Purchases

Sales

Stock

CASH

Raw Materials

Process

W.I.P. — *Process*

Payments
Repayments
Investments

7: FINANCIAL MODELLING

In addition, you need to:

- Demonstrate tight control over costs vis-a-vis income
- Demonstrate that you can service debt
- Provide an adequate return on invested capital
- Retain earnings for growth

You must, therefore, produce financial models to support these, including:

- Cashflow forecasts
- Projected profit and loss
- Expected balance sheets
- Funds flow statement

The latter three statements are probably inappropriate for internal departments. Many organisations produce cashflows on a regular basis (weekly) for management purposes.

7: FINANCIAL MODELLING

CASHFLOW FORECASTS

- These are estimates of the likely expenditure and receipts in cash terms over the next 12 months.

- Cashflow is vital to a business and anyone looking either to lend, invest or extend credit to you will wish to see that the business can generate sufficient cash to cover its outgoings.

- An accurate cashflow will enable you to predict your financing needs, allowing you to establish facilities in advance when lenders are more sympathetic, rather than afterwards, when they will be less so.

- Producing a cashflow forecast allows you to demonstrate that you have thought through the flows of cash (not funds or profit). Interested parties can then challenge your assumptions; your answers to these challenges will give them confidence that the assumptions, and therefore the forecast, are likely to prove robust.

7: FINANCIAL MODELLING

CASHFLOW FORECAST : EXAMPLE

MONTH ▶	1	2	3	4	5	6	7	8	9	10	11	12
Opening balance	xx	45	72	96	(123)	50	83	87	(123)	67	96	123
Receipts	XX	XX	XX	XX	XX	XX	XX	XX	XX	XX	XX	XX
Debtors	XX	XX	XX	XX	XX	XX	XX	XX	XX	XX	XX	XX
Assets sales	XX	XX	XX	XX	XX	XX	XX	XX	XX	XX	XX	XX
Capital injection	XX	XX	XX	XX	XX	XX	XX	XX	XX	XX	XX	XX
Interest received	XX	XX	XX	XX	XX	XX	XX	XX	XX	XX	XX	XX
Dividends received	XX	XX	XX	XX	XX	XX	XX	XX	XX	XX	XX	XX
Expenditure	XX	XX	XX	XX	XX	XX	XX	XX	XX	XX	XX	XX
Salaries	XX	XX	XX	XX	XX	XX	XX	XX	XX	XX	XX	XX
Rent	XX	XX	XX	XX	XX	XX	XX	XX	XX	XX	XX	XX
Rates	XX	XX	XX	XX	XX	XX	XX	XX	XX	XX	XX	XX
Assets purchase	XX	XX	XX	XX	XX	XX	XX	XX	XX	XX	XX	XX
Creditors	XX	XX	XX	XX	XX	XX	XX	XX	XX	XX	XX	XX
Tax	XX	XX	XX	XX	XX	XX	XX	XX	XX	XX	XX	XX
Drawings/dividends	XX	XX	XX	XX	XX	XX	XX	XX	XX	XX	XX	XX
Closing balance	45	72	96	(123)	50	83	87	(123)	67	96	123	48

This enables financing needs (months 4 and 8) to be predicted and catered for in advance.

7: FINANCIAL MODELLING

PROFIT & LOSS

This is a statement of the historical performance of a business or unit in terms of:

- Its annual revenue and the key components
- The costs associated with that revenue and the major categories
- The resulting profit (gross and net)
- How the profit was apportioned (paid out as dividends, placed into reserves for future growth, etc)

It serves as a useful financial statement for assessment of past performance as well as extrapolated likely future trends.

Producing a forecast profit and loss as part of your plan will demonstrate the impact of the plan in financial performance terms.

Internal/support departments will not usually have them.

7: FINANCIAL MODELLING

PROFIT & LOSS: EXAMPLE

INCOME STATEMENT

	£m
TURNOVER	107.0
Less	
Cost of sales	32.0
Distribution costs	13.0
Administration costs	27.0
Plus	
Other operating income	11.0
Adjustments	(3.0)
TRADING PROFIT	43.0
Associated co's profits	2.0
PROFIT BEFORE INTEREST & TAX	45.0
Net interest payable(+/-)	(13.0)
PROFIT BEFORE TAX	32.0
Tax payable	(17.0)
PROFIT AFTER TAX	15.0
Minorities	–
Extraordinaries	(5.0)
NET PROFIT	10.0
Dividends	4.0
PROFIT RETAINED	6.0

7: FINANCIAL MODELLING
BALANCE SHEET

The balance sheet is a 'snapshot' of an organisation's position as at a given date (usually the end of a year, either fiscal or actual).

It shows:

- The **assets** of an organisation - what it **owns**

- The **liabilities** of an organisation - what it **owes**

- The difference is what an organisation is worth - often called **equity, shareholders' net worth**, etc

Although only a picture of one day, it does nevertheless give valuable information as to component parts of an organisation.

A good plan will often include a forecast balance sheet to demonstrate the impacts on asset and liabilities. Many organisations produce this on a regular basis (weekly) for management purposes.

7: FINANCIAL MODELLING

BALANCE SHEET : EXAMPLE

£ m

50	Current assets	(cash, investments, debtors, stock, prepayments)
	Less	
(25)	Current liabilities	(tax, creditors, S/T debt, dividends)
15	**Net working capital**	
	Plus	
100	Fixed assets	(plant, machinery, land and buildings, IT, etc)
	Less	
(70)	Creditors	(loans, long-term creditors, deferred tax)
45	**Net assets**	
	financed by	
45	**Shareholders' net worth**	(capital, retained profit, reserves)

7: FINANCIAL MODELLING

SOURCES & USES OF FUNDS

This statement shows how an organisation funded itself through the year. In particular it shows:

- Where the money came from
- Where it went
- The duration of the funds in
- The maturity of funds out (to allow mismatch analysis)

It is self-evident that sources and uses should by and large reflect the same timescale. It would be very foolish to borrow short-term (less than three months or even overnight) to fund a long-term (eg: five year) project. Interest rates would probably move against you, maturity of outflows would almost certainly occur at unfavourable times, and you might be unable to fund the project at any given time if there was a credit squeeze.

Demonstrating that this aspect has been considered goes a long way to instilling confidence in you and your plan.

PLANNING PROCESS

7: FINANCIAL MODELLING
SOURCES & USES STATEMENT

Sources	Applications/uses
• Pre-tax profit	• Dividends paid/drawings
• Depreciation	• Tax payments
• Sales of assets	• Loan repayments
• Decrease in stocks	• Decrease in creditors
• Decrease in debtors	• Increase in stocks
• Shares issued	• Increase in debtors
• Increased loans	• Purchase of assets
• Increased creditors	

7: FINANCIAL MODELLING

SOURCES & USES

Key points - there are only four sources of funds:

- Cashflow from operations
- Asset sales
- Capital injection
- Debt

Funds will not come from anywhere else, so any funding must be explained in these terms. Anyone looking at the plan will give especial attention to funding, as it is a lack of this that causes problems.

This statement provides the link between the opening balance sheet, the profit and loss for the period and the closing balance sheet.

Sources of funds are increases in liabilities (increase in borrowing/capital) or decreases in assets (release of funds, use of cash), **Applications of funds** are decreases in liabilities (repayments/payments) or increases in assets (purchases or extra cash).

NOTES

PRACTICAL PLANNING

STRUCTURING A PLAN

When assembling a plan, you must think of those reading it - whether your colleagues, superiors, investors, creditors or suppliers.

- Does it say what you want it to say, in the best manner, portraying your organisation in the best light, truthfully but giving your readers the information that they need?

- Is all relevant information present and in an easily digestible form?

- Is there a logical flow?

- Does it support your objectives?

Wherever possible, detail should be in appendices so as not to detract from the key messages, and to provide clarity and ease of reading.

STRUCTURING A PLAN

Typical structure of a plan would be as follows:

- Summary
- Introduction and description of the business
- Market analysis
- Internal situation analysis
- Marketing plan
- Operational plan
- Financials
- Resource requirements
- Appendices

An example using a company for illustration follows on the next few pages.

PRACTICAL PLANNING

EXAMPLE COMPANY

The example company operates in the brewing industry.

- It has a turnover of £150 million
- It has 80 employees
- The board consists of five executive directors (family) and three non-executives
- It has just introduced a role of planner, and put in hand a planning process, having undergone a strategic review last year
- It is based in the north of England where its market is primarily located

The example is fictitious but intended to illustrate a plan. In the following pages extracts from its plan are shown.

STRUCTURING A PLAN

STYLE OF SUMMARY

- The key objective is to get the readers' attention and to make them wish to read on

- For very large organisations, the summary may itself be quite lengthy, in other firms quite short

- It should, however, be a stand-alone document which takes the readers by the hand and leads them to support the conclusion that you have drawn

- Many people will read nothing else, but the rest of the plan should support the summary, allowing them to 'drill down' for information

STRUCTURING A PLAN
BREWING COMPANY SUMMARY

* Increase market share by 3% in draught beer, 5% in bottled beer and 7% in soft drinks

* Absolute increase in sales by 12%, improved profits by 20% (from market penetration and reduced costs)

* Replace general ledger with new package

* Outsource distribution

STRUCTURING A PLAN
INTRODUCTION

Description of the organisation/unit

The company is engaged in brewing and the supply of ancillary products such as soft drinks, spirits, etc.

It is split into four departments:

* Brewing (which makes the beer)
* Sales and marketing (which ensures it is sold)
* Distribution (which delivers supplies)
* Head office support (finance - including planning - HR, IT) which provides infrastructure support
* All operations are located on one site
* It has its own transport fleet
* etc

BETTER BEERS

STRUCTURING A PLAN

MARKET ANALYSIS

The market is dominated by three very large brewers with a few middle-sized, largely regional companies, and several small organisations catering for local areas or specialised beers.

* The industry's tied sales have been reduced drastically through legal requirements resulting in the emergence of several large independent chains of outlets

* The home sales market has increased substantially in recent years through supermarkets, which has radically changed the distribution dynamics and forced down prices

* Profits have been hit accordingly

* Profits are further under pressure from premium bottled imported beers which have eaten into the traditional draught market

* etc

STRUCTURING A PLAN

MARKETING PLAN

BETTER BEERS

Overall objectives:

* To increase sales in home consumption market by 15%
* As a minimum, retain position in free houses and increase throughput by 5%
* Introduce two new beer products this year and one soft drink
* Expand geographical market into one new region - Scotland
* Tie up an agreement with local supermarket chain
* Sponsor one or two key local events
* etc

STRUCTURING A PLAN

OPERATIONAL PLAN

BETTER
BEERS

Given the pressures within the market,
operations must:

* Increase efficiency by investing in new brewing plant
* Reduce operating costs by 25% or better
* Put in hand plans for the outsourcing of distribution over the next two years
* Reduce brewing/delivery cycles by 10%
* etc

STRUCTURING A PLAN
RESOURCE REQUIREMENTS

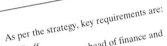

As per the strategy, key requirements are:

 BETTER BEERS

* Staff
  - appoint a new head of finance and administration
  - recruit a planner
  - recruit a new regional marketing director for Scotland
* Capital investment
  - replace existing plant
  - if Scottish sales targets are made, consider buying site north of the border for administration and storage/distribution
* IT
  - replace existing legacy system (finance and general ledger) with package
  - ensure systems are euro compliant

* etc

PRACTICAL PLANNING

STRUCTURING A PLAN
APPENDICES

BETTER BEERS

* Marketing report on brewing industry to year 2010
* HR report into skills and training requirements
* Financials (P & L, Balance Sheet, Sources and Uses, Cashflow, Ratio Analysis)
* IT review
* Annual sales report, including product profitability analysis
* Distribution schedules for previous year
* etc

COMMUNICATING A PLAN

It is up to you to make sure that your plan communicates well to the reader. Each reader will have different needs, albeit with a high degree of commonality.

You should decide on whether you need to prepare different versions for different audiences.

COMMUNICATING A PLAN
THE PYRAMID

In communicating a plan, remember to make your message stand out.

Adopt a pyramidal approach:

- Key message in the summary
- Supporting points in the main body
- Real details in the appendices
- Allow readers to drill down to the level they require
- Summary is a stand-alone document

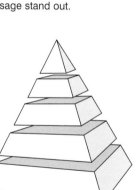

PRACTICAL PLANNING

COMMUNICATING A PLAN

You must tailor the level of information to ensure that you hold attention. Do not clutter it with inessential detail.

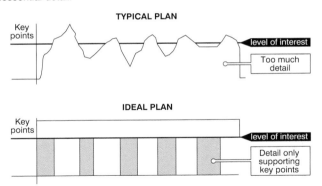

PRACTICAL PLANNING

USING A PLAN

A plan is **of no use whatsoever unless it is used**. This means that the theoretical thinking must be translated into something tangible - **action**.

The plan is only a route map and must be used as such. On a regular basis you must take time to look at where you are and compare and contrast your position with what you had planned. You should then take action to put yourself back on course if you are adrift, to change course if events demand it, or alter the plan to reflect reality.

Typically, given that a plan is short-term, most measurement against it tends to be budgetary variance analysis, and subsequent investigation into the reasons. However, the plan was prepared to indicate your intentions for the future, and as such should be used in the same way as you might use a road map. Consult the plan regularly to ensure that you are following the steps - they will usually have been the output of much thought and deliberation and will help you.

PRACTICAL PLANNING

USING A PLAN

To ensure maximum use of your plan it is very important to take regular stock of where you are. This usually involves preparing a report indicating current progress and reasons for non-achievement. Depending on the type of business, you will either review this yourself (sole trader, partner, small business) or present it at a more formal forum, eg: monthly management meetings. Typical contents of a report would be:

- Management summary
- Profit and Loss account; this month and YTD
- Balance sheet; this month and YTD
- Analysis of business area performance
- Expense analysis
- Sales commentary
- Revised year end forecasts
- Capital utilisation
- Actions for next period

PRACTICAL PLANNING

CONTINGENCY PLANNING

Rarely does everything go according to plan. Consequently you must look at potential problems and develop a strategy for dealing with them. It is not the **expected problems** that cause difficulties, but rather the **unexpected ones**.

A good way to plan for contingencies is to contrast the **probability** of an event with the **magnitude** of damage it is likely to inflict. For example, an employee is likely to be sick occasionally but this should not have serious implications unless that person has an indispensable role.

Here's another example: an earthquake could devastate a business but is unlikely to occur in, say, the UK. You would, therefore, grade the severity of the event as 6 and the likelihood as 1, giving a risk weighting of 6 (action: 'ignore'). In California, however, the severity could be 8, the likelihood 8 and the risk weighting, therefore, 64 (action: 'take considerable steps to address the problem').

The chart on the next page shows one organisation's analysis and weighting of risks.

PRACTICAL PLANNING

RISK ASSESSMENT MATRIX

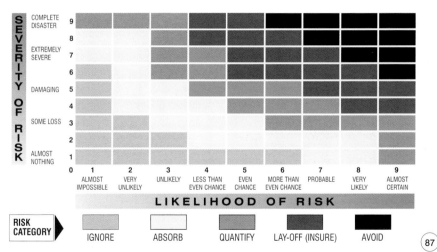

PRACTICAL PLANNING

CONTINGENCY PLANNING

There are many events that can have adverse impacts on your business - they will depend upon the exact nature of your markets and the supply chain, environment, etc. Below is a list of some of these; however, it is neither exhaustive nor exclusive so you must think them through for yourself and ensure that your plan addresses them:

- Strikes - your own staff or suppliers, distributors
- Price war - in your market or suppliers, substitute goods
- Legislation change - positive or negative
- Change of government
- Embargo - goods in or out
- Plant failure
- Fire
- Inflation
- Currency fluctuations
- Technological obsolescence
- 'Shocks' - eg: oil price rise in 70s or the terrible events of September 11th 2001

PRACTICAL PLANNING

ORGANISING TO PLAN

The way you organise for your planning will vary depending on the type and size
of the organisation:

- Sole traders will often do it themselves; perhaps with the help of a financial adviser

- A unit manager will plan him/herself, perhaps involving key staff

- Very large organisations often have planning departments, not to mention
  cumbersome time-consuming processes

- Others are totally decentralised

- Some have small central bodies which carry out forecasting, macro-economic
  analysis and set group targets; which are then cascaded down the organisation
  to form planning frameworks

PRACTICAL PLANNING

ORGANISING TO PLAN

- Clearly you will have to work within your constraints but you should try to produce a plan using the minimum resources to carry out a cost-effective job

- Whilst successful organisations tend to spend more time planning than those that are unsuccessful, the law of diminishing returns sets in quite quickly

- The style of planning should fit in with your organisation and reflect the way it works

PRACTICAL PLANNING

ORGANISING TO PLAN

Typical planning hierarchy in a large organisation

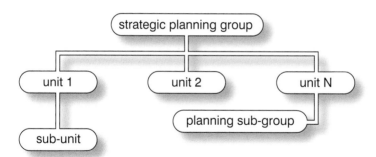

PRACTICAL PLANNING

PLANNING CYCLE

Every organisation will have a different planning cycle driven by the fiscal needs, the type of organisation and the type of planning in use. Usually, however, the planning cycle is the same each year. A typical cycle would be as follows:

- Central unit(s) carry out socio-political economic forecasts to review trends that will impact the business

- Based on these, guidelines will be set for the units

- The strategy will be reviewed for any changes as a result of shifts in the environment

- This will be communicated along with the guidelines, last year's plans and results as well as dates for submission of this year's plan

- Units prepare their plans and budgets and a process of review and iteration takes place

- The final plans are agreed and signed off in time for the next year

Typical timings are shown on the next page.

PRACTICAL PLANNING

PLANNING CYCLE

Planning cycle timings - example

- Central units will carry out socio-political forecasts to review trends that will impact the business

- Two months or so prior to the end of the current planning cycle

- Based on these, guidelines will be set for units

- One month or so prior to the end of the current planning year

- The strategy will be reviewed for any changes due to shifts in the assumptions/environment

- One month or so prior to the end of the current planning year

- This will be communicated along with the guidelines, last year's plans and results as well as timings for submission of this year's plan

- One to two months into the new planning year

- Units prepare their plans and budgets and an iterative process of analysis and challenge followed by amendments, etc, takes place

- Three to six months into the new planning year

- The final plans are agreed and signed off in time for next year

- Six to ten months into the new year

PRACTICAL PLANNING

PLANNING TOOLS & TECHNIQUES
TIMECHARTS

Almost all plans will contain a timechart of some sort. This links tasks with time and often shows dependencies. Usually, it will detail resources and critical elements.

There are several types of these ranging from the familiar bar charts through to more qualitative examples, although they are all designed to give the same output - a route map of the way forward. Two of the more usual are:

● Gantt charts

● PERT analysis

Both of which are different ways of showing Critical Path Management (CPM).

PLANNING TOOLS & TECHNIQUES

CRITICAL PATH MANAGEMENT

Critical Path Management (CPM), also known as Critical Path Analysis (CPA), was developed to help manage very complicated projects. The principles on which it is based, however, are very relevant to planning. These are:

- In all sets of actions (which is what a plan is) there are a number which are both critical and on which others are dependent, ie: without them either key parts of the plan do not happen or other parts cannot take place until they are finished

- By identifying these actions - known as the critical path - it is possible to chart the minimum time to complete

- Once they are identified, contingency action can be formulated to 'crash' parts of the plan where possible (eg: by throwing more resources at it) to speed up some parts

- Whole sets of actions can be further broken down and sub-sets of critical paths identified (eg: for planning purposes the strategy would contain IT, marketing, manpower plans, etc)

PRACTICAL PLANNING

PLANNING TOOLS & TECHNIQUES
GANTT CHARTS

A GANTT chart is a series of bar charts showing the relative timings of a set of tasks. It will usually show performance time and elapsed time and might well also include resources (man days) and costs. It can be in a very simple form, or very complex and the output of a computer programme.

It is often used for project management, but serves equally well to demonstrate how a plan will look, as all plans are sets of tasks to be carried out. The level of detail depends on the complexity of the plan.

Where the chart is produced from a computer, it can also be used to chart slippages, carry out 'what if?' analysis and measure progress.

(See diagram opposite)

PLANNING TOOLS & TECHNIQUES

GANTT CHART : EXAMPLE

ID	Task Name	Dur-ation	Start	December					January				February		
				30/11	07/12	14/12	21/12	28/12	04/01	11/01	18/01	25/01	01/02	08/02	15/02
1	commence planning cycle	60d	Sun 30/11/02												
2	collect economic data	20d	Mon 01/12/02												
3	obtain final sign-off to last year's budget	0d	Sun 30/11/02	○ 30/11/02 08:00											
4	analyse	35d	Fri 21/01/03												
5	prepare assumptions for planning	25d	Tue 02/12/02												
6	obtain sign-off	0d	Mon 05/01/03						○ 05/01/03 17:00						
7	circulate to managers	5d	Tue 06/01/03												
8	develop budget guidelines	25d	Tue 02/12/02												
9	send out to managers	5d	Mon 16/02/03												
10	develop corporate targets	35d	Mon 29/12/02												

Milestone

97

PRACTICAL PLANNING

PLANNING TOOLS & TECHNIQUES
PERT ANALYSIS

PERT (which stands for Project Evaluation Resource Techniques) is another form of planning which focuses on the tasks that must be carried out and the relationship between them.

It shows dependencies and measures the critical path, ie: those tasks which must be carried out to ensure that the end objectives are reached. It was developed for very complex projects such as building submarines, etc, but can be used to provide a visual representation of the relationships between a set of tasks in any plan. It gives information by task such as task number, time to complete, which tasks precede and which follow, as well as start and end dates.

It is particularly useful in that it identifies those tasks critical to success and enables you to model what happens if they change.

(See diagram opposite)

PLANNING TOOLS & TECHNIQUES

PERT CHART

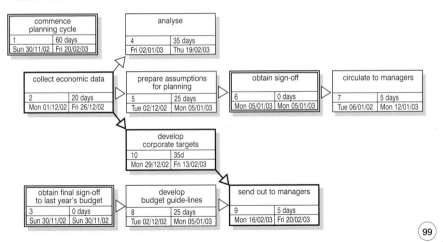

commence planning cycle		
1	60 days	
Sun 30/11/02	Fri 20/02/03	

analyse		
4	35 days	
Fri 02/01/03	Thu 19/02/03	

collect economic data		
2	20 days	
Mon 01/12/02	Fri 26/12/02	

prepare assumptions for planning		
5	25 days	
Tue 02/12/02	Mon 05/01/03	

obtain sign-off		
6	0 days	
Mon 05/01/03	Mon 05/01/03	

circulate to managers		
7	5 days	
Tue 06/01/02	Mon 12/01/03	

develop corporate targets		
10	35d	
Mon 29/12/02	Fri 13/02/03	

obtain final sign-off to last year's budget		
3	0 days	
Sun 30/11/02	Sun 30/11/02	

develop budget guide-lines		
8	25 days	
Tue 02/12/02	Mon 05/01/03	

send out to managers		
9	5 days	
Mon 16/02/03	Fri 20/02/03	

99

PRACTICAL PLANNING

TIPS

When planning, there are a few key points to bear in mind:

- Don't make the plan over-optimistic, especially with regard to sales; this is very common

- Set realistic and achievable targets

- Don't underestimate financing requirements, it is much harder to go back later on and ask for more - it undermines credibility in your planning; you couldn't get that right, why should you be right about anything else?

- Think through your plan at a high level before committing to paper; the objectives, key tasks, timings, resources, etc

- Write the summary last - it should be just that

- Make sure that your numbers add up and cross-cast; errors there undermine credibility

- Don't be afraid to change the plan if circumstances change radically, but also try to plan for changes

PRACTICAL PLANNING

TIPS

- **Start early** - time disappears faster than you think
- **Involve the right people** - they will not buy-in if they have not been consulted
- **Discuss** it with affected parties prior to finalisation
- **Be concise** - remember KISS
- **Make sure** that it supports the overall plan
- Only **analyse** what is relevant (Pareto's Law*)
- Where data is unavailable, either **commission research** (expensive) or **make supportable assumptions**
- **State** any assumptions in the introduction
- **Put details** in appendices
- **Write** with the ultimate reader in mind; will he/she understand it
- **Be realistic and get help** where you need it

* 80:20 rule: 20% of analysis will yield 80% of results

BUSINESS PLANNING

SUMMARY

A plan is a statement of what you intend to achieve, how, when and with what resources:

- It will contain targets against which to measure success
- It is a communication tool to interested parties
- It should focus on the key issues, with supporting detail as appropriate
- It should demonstrate forethought and contingency consideration
- It must be realistic, pragmatic and flexible
- It should support the strategy

About the Author

Neil Russell-Jones MBA is a management consultant. He is
a chartered banker and a member of the Strategic Planning
Society. He has worked internationally with many
organisations, particularly in the areas of strategy, BPR,
change management and shareholder value. He is a guest
lecturer on the City University Business School's Evening
MBA Programme and has lectured and spoken in many
countries. He is also an advisor for The Prince's Trust. The
numerous articles and books written by him include three
other pocketbooks (on decision-making, marketing and
managing change), 'Financial Services – 1992' (Eurostudy)
and 'Marketing for Success' and 'Value Pricing',
both published by Kogan Page and written in conjunction
with Dr Tony Fletcher.

Contact: you can reach Neil on this e-mail:
neiljones@neilsweb.fsnet.co.uk

MARKETING
Pocketbook

A pocketful of tips, techniques and tools for all those involved in the marketing process - research, strategy, planning and tactics

Neil Russell-Jones & Tony Fletcher

Other Pocketbooks by the author include:

The Managing Change Pocketbook, The Decision-making Pocketbook
and **The Marketing Pocketbook** (illustrated).

BALANCE SHEET
Pocketbook

A pocketful of guidance
and advice to help explain
profit and loss reports,
balance sheets and the
way money works
within business

Anne Hawkins &
Clive Turner

Pocketbook titles in the Finance Series are:

The Balance Sheet Pocketbook (illustrated), **The Managing Cashflow Pocketbook**,
The Managing Budgets Pocketbook and **The Improving Profitability Pocketbook**.

THE MANAGEMENT POCKETBOOK SERIES

Pocketbooks

Appraisals
Assertiveness
Balance Sheet
Business Planning
Business Presenter's
Business Writing
Career Transition
Challengers
Coaching
Communicator's
Controlling Absenteeism
Creative Manager's
C.R.M.
Cross-cultural Business
Cultural Gaffes
Customer Service
Decision-making
Developing People
Discipline
Diversity
E-commerce
E-customer Care

Emotional Intelligence
Employment Law
Empowerment
Energy and Well-being
Facilitator's
Handling Complaints
Icebreakers
Improving Efficiency
Improving Profitability
Induction
Influencing
International Trade
Interviewer's
I.T. Trainer's
Key Account Manager's
Leadership
Learner's
Manager's
Managing Budgets
Managing Cashflow
Managing Change
Managing Upwards

Managing Your Appraisal
Marketing
Meetings
Mentoring
Motivation
Negotiator's
Networking
People Manager's
Performance Management
Personal Success
Project Management
Problem Behaviour
Problem Solving
Quality
Resolving Conflict
Sales Excellence
Salesperson's
Self-managed Development
Starting In Management
Stress
Succeeding at Interviews
Teamworking

Telephone Skills
Telesales
Thinker's
Time Management
Trainer Standards
Trainer's

Pocketsquares

Great Training Robbery
Hook Your Audience
Leadership: Sharing The Passion

Pocketfiles

Trainer's Blue Pocketfile of
Ready-to-use Exercises

Trainer's Green Pocketfile of
Ready-to-use Exercises

Trainer's Red Pocketfile of
Ready-to-use Exercises

ORDER FORM

Your details

Name _____

Position _____

Company _____

Address _____

_____

Telephone _____

Facsimile _____

E-mail _____

VAT No. (EC companies) _____

Your Order Ref _____

Please send me:

			No. copies
The	Business Planning	Pocketbook	☐
The	_____	Pocketbook	☐
The	_____	Pocketbook	☐
The	_____	Pocketbook	☐
The	_____	Pocketbook	☐

Order by Post

MANAGEMENT POCKETBOOKS LTD

LAUREL HOUSE, STATION APPROACH, ALRESFORD,
HAMPSHIRE SO24 9JH UK

Order by Phone, Fax or Internet

Telephone: +44 (0)1962 735573
Facsimile: +44 (0)1962 733637
E-mail: sales@pocketbook.co.uk
Web: www.pocketbook.co.uk

Customers in USA should contact:
Stylus Publishing, LLC, 22883 Quicksilver Drive,
Sterling, VA 20166-2012
Telephone: 703 661 1581 or 800 232 0223
Facsimile: 703 661 1501 E-mail: styluspub@aol.com

'Words

that

speak

volumes'

MANAGEMENT
POCKETBOOKS

RESOLVING CONFLICT
Pocketbook

MANAGER'S
Pocketbook

INTERVIEWER'S
Pocketbook

IMPACT & PRESENCE
Pocketbook

A pocketful of
tips, tools and
techniques on how to
create 'brand you', build
leadership presence and
achieve impact

Pam Jones &
Jane Van Hool

Coventry University